THERE WAS A TIME

THERE WAS A TIME

Volume II
1988 and 1989

Arthur R. Marinello

Copyright © 2019 by Arthur R. Marinello

ISBN: 978-1-63522-008-7

Printed in the United States of America
10   9   8   7   6   5   4   3   2   1

RIVERSHORE BOOKS

Rivershore Books
8982 Van Buren St. NE • Minneapolis, MN 55434
763-670-8677 • info@rivershorebooks.com

DEDICATION

For my beloved

PREFACE

Writing the lines contained in this volume has been, despite the pain associated with the subject, in some cases, a singular pleasure of creative expression. All that we do is art, but some art is practiced with an accompanying awareness of its blessed nature.

Making furniture, cleaning house, cooking a meal, baking - - - - - - all is art - - - - and fortunate is the person who is aware of it.

Arthur R. Marinello
December 27, 1989
North Hollywood

TABLE OF CONTENTS

THE SWIMMING POOL

Thursday, March 17, 1988

This morning I found myself
Taking a swim in the small pool
Of the motel we were staying at
In Ventura

We had gone there for a few days
To try to deal with the allergy problem
Which has been a source of discomfort
And, at times, extreme suffering,
For my wife.

It may or may not have worked.
It isn't clear.
This kind of thing - - - - - -
Has that way about it.
We may know better
After a while.

But it was nice to get away.
It was generally beneficial.
The phone was present
But not oppressive
Not demanding.

We had complimentary breakfasts.
We had lunch in our motel room twice.
And the meals out were interesting.

We went to daily Mass at the Mission.
We visited with the Bushes.
We became better acquainted
With the town, currently said
To have a population of seventy thousand.
We walked on the beach.

After this morning's walk, on the beach,
I was reminded that I had planned
To take a swim in the heated pool,
At the motel.

And so, soon after,
I found myself braving the elevator
And the motel lobby and dining room.
In my bathing trunks, plus towel.
Very few people were about - - - -

In another moment, I was in the pool
The sun shining overhead.
I found myself singing out loud.
O Sole Mio.
No one else was there.

I kept singing and singing
And enjoying it.
And I felt, again, the gratitude
For this heritage
Which my mother left me.
She of the singing mornings.
Those mornings in the summer
When school was out
And I could stay late in bed
Not getting up 'til mid-morning
When I would waken to her singing.
She'd be singing Neapolitan love songs,
In the kitchen.
It was a pleasant enough experience
For me - - - - - then.
A luxuriant one, perhaps,
When I had no idea that the merits
Of that experience
Would be understated
If revalued a hundred-fold.
Because, in fact, I have many times
These past years
Considered the joy of the memory itself - - -
The feeling
The blessedness
The blessings multiplied.

She may have gone many years ago
But her songs are sung by me
To my grandson, Vincent,
Whose appreciative listening
Has a quality of enthrallment, at times,
Which is inexplicable, I think,
By this world's understanding.

She may be gone these many years
But her singing - - - - - her songs - - -
Are, to me, tangible evidence of her presence,
Then, and now.

Give or take a few years,
She would have been forty, in those days
That I remember her singing.

And she sang because she sang.
She sang not to be remembered
Fifty-five years later,
But because she sang the songs
That a Neapolitan would sing,
Because her heart could not help but sing
Like others from her homeland
Who sing with love and joy and wonderment
No matter the pain and melancholy.

It's been said before, in various ways,
That what we do, sometimes,
No matter how little noticed by ourselves
Can have a lasting impression - - - - -
On someone else.
I've seen examples of this.

Human existence is, perforce, a busy existence - - -
By its very nature.
Even quietly we exist.
Even quietly we are active.
Always we exist.
Even in death.

For good or ill, our influence is great.
Great in that it can have bearing
On some other human life
And each life so precious.

When we do harm to others
Through this mechanism of influence
With ourselves the actors upon others
Whose dependence and receptivity
Whose impressionableness at a tender stage in life
Makes them victims
We must be forgiven
For truly, we know not what we do.

And when, somehow, what we do, does good - - -
When midst the incalculable harm,
The evil that persists,
From generation to generation - - -
When, somehow, inexplicably, there is good - - -
Innocent joy
A laugh
A song
The appreciation of its merit
Can be so intense
As to be wordless.

Blessedness is all.

ON GRADUATING FROM THE UNIVERSITY

Saturday, June 11, 1988

Andy,
I don't think you should be
Congratulated
Because the road was long.
It was only moderately so.
After all, you're only thirty.
Nor because it was difficult,
Academically speaking,
Though it was moderately so,
Given your gifts.
After all,
You made some detours along the way.
They were your choices,
And, along the way,
We were all in there with you - - -
Suffering, usually.
Especially knowing
You had it in you.
So, no congratulations for that.

But, Andy
There's something else here.
Surely, congratulations for being able
To start on a path
You should find more rewarding
Plus a sense of freedom to change
To something else
Now that you will have passed the test.

But more than that - - - -
Congratulations - - - -
That your faith in yourself
And in those around you - - -
And beyond - - -
To the unknown
And the little known
Has reached this stage of fruition
And that,
The future promises - - - - -
More of the same.

love,

Mom and Dad

SUFFERING

Wednesday, June 15, 1988

It seems that no one wants to suffer.
It seems that for many people
The goal is to get through this life
Without suffering
Of any kind.

How can this be?
How did this come about?
When all around us - - - - -
There is suffering
And pain.

We have made ourselves,
In varying degrees,
Into people
Running from pain.

Running and casting off,
What we cannot outdistance
We wish to cast off,
Somehow,
Even onto someone else.

Why is suffering so hard to bear?
Is it simply that?
Too much to bear?
But surely we can.
No suffering is likely to be more
Than we can take.

The most grievous pain,
Given to the weakest among us,
Has been borne
Has even been accepted
Has been shouldered
And carried.

There must be something
In our view of life
Which enlarges on the pain
And, at the same time,
Underestimates our strength - - - -
Our capacity to suffer.

And when we feel overwhelmed
By our suffering and pain
We must fall, or run,
Or cast off the load - - - -
Onto someone else.

Someone else has a lighter burden
Or seems to.
Someone else is to blame
Or seems to be.
Someone else has the strength
Or seems to.
Someone else may be blaming us
Or seems to.

PRAYING

Friday, July 8, 1988

Lord, I come to you as a child
And you answer me.
Unabashed in my humility,
And you reward me.
When I am distressed
You give me calm.
A font of goodness - - -
Waiting.

What I must do is take the step;
Know the road,
The question.
Ask - - -
And wait.

Is there a limit to the number of questions
For a certain span of time?
Is there a limit to the requests
That will be responded to?
An irrelevant question, perhaps,
When my own capacity to ask
Has been blocked by barriers
Of every sort.

UNIQUE

Wednesday, September 7, 1988

Lord, you have made it so difficult
All this uniqueness,
This free will.

How can we understand one another
When we hardly know ourselves
So complex are we.

How can we understand one another
When the model we would work from
Is ourselves
And we are so unique
And yet would fit others
Into the same mold as ours,
And fail,
Repeatedly - - - -
As we must.

FOR STEVE ON HIS 34TH BIRTHDAY, FEBRUARY 5, 1989

Monday, January 30, 1989

You were born on a Saturday afternoon
You were not quite ready, at first,
So, the doctor waited.
Welch was his name,
Of the team of Welch and Culbertson.

Grandma was at home with your sister.
We lived in Pomona then
And the hospital was in Pomona - - - -
Making you the only one
To be born in the same town
We were living in.

For the first three months,
Miraculously,
You slept through each night.
But that was all.
After that, you developed the routine
                we knew so well
Waking at all hours.

As a small child you were alert, eager, daring.
(Although you could explore cautiously.)
When you were eight months old
The back of the potty chair fell with a bang,
Heavy wood it was,
And it startled you.
Immediately, you raised and dropped it - - - -
Repeatedly.

At eleven months, you were running from
                    the kitchen (in Pomona)
Into the living room - - - eagerly - - -
With a cup in your hand - - - - and fell - - - -
With the base of your nose colliding - - - -
          with the rim of the cup.

Some time later, on a Sunday, - - - in Pomona - - -
(We alternated Sunday dinners with your
                    uncle Joe - - - in those days.)
They came to our house.
Again, eagerly, you ran to greet them
And the kitchen door slammed you in the face.
Aunt Julie was the unwitting agent of this mishap.
(You were two and a half when we moved from
                    Pomona to North Hollywood.)

Very early on, at your baptism, at St. Joseph's
                    in Pomona
(You were a month old.)
With Aunt Julie holding you.
(In those days we were under the impression that
          custom dictated that mothers not
                    be present at their children's
                              baptisms.)
You raised holy hell throughout.

You were always eager and alert
Ever on the cutting edge - - - intelligent.
Our puzzlement and consternation,
Mingled with the activity, pride and enjoyment
That went with raising each and all of you - - -
Began to receive a beam of light
When, in second or third grade
The psychologist at school, a tall colored fellow,
Called us in to report, amazed and ecstatic,
That he had tested and found you highly gifted.

As the years went by
The rest of you were classified as gifted
And yet another insight came to me
Some ten years ago,
When Dolores Sherlock noted that each of you
                        was gifted
Whereas only one of hers, Kevin, was.

I think you'll agree,
Especially using Kevin as an example,
That giftedness - - - -
Is a mixed blessing.
Along with the obvious benefits,
It carries, for parents, both pain and peril.
In fact, or so it seems,
The whole business is of doubtful value,
Operating, probably most of the time - - - -
In most cases, that is,
In a terribly negative and harmful manner.

You're fortunate that you possess a certain humility,
Indiscernible to some,
Which tempers one of the pitfalls of a quick mind - - -
                        arrogance, impatience.
You're lucky to have an abundance of energy
Which counteracts another danger - - - laziness.
You're blessed to have not only faith - - - -
                        but renewable faith - - - -
                    to oppose cynicism.

You could use a greater sense of political expediency
An earlier warning and corrective action system
To minimize the disappointments we all of us face
To enable you to chuck the bad that comes your way
To cut the costs, the burdens, when you persist for
                more time than it's worth.
But then, again, you're only thirty-four today,
Just half my age.
Time to say - - - Happy Birthday,
And a happy next thirty-four,
Because life is good.

                        love,

                        Mom and Dad

MY FATHER

Tuesday, March 7, 1989

How could I have forgotten how important my father was?
He was the whole world to us.
He was the whole world to me - - -
The rock.

Could I have been so stunned
By his crumbling,
By the great loss of him who was so indispensable,
That I would relegate him to an area
                    of silence - - -
                        in my life?

Were his shortcomings so grave
That he should be set aside?
I think not - - -
I, who haven't given the matter proper thought.

What did he do that was so condemnable?
Did he not simply fall
Under the weight of burdens and the onslaught
            of demons and phantoms
Too much for him to bear?

And, did I not learn from him?
Did I not learn, even from his failures?
Did I not learn to be strong where he was not.
Did I not learn patience where he had not.
Did I not learn flexibility where he had not.

Did I not learn, likewise,
To take the long view - - -
To make provision - - - -
To recognize my worth - - -
To place the well-being of myself first
For in that well-being is the hope and the
                welfare of my family - - -
                        my wife and children?

Did I not learn all this from him
And did I not learn these things
                because I was so much with
                        him - - - in spirit
Because all his failures, his turmoil,
                his tragic end
Were all within me.
I lived it as it happened.

How could I have forgotten?
Or, rather, how could I have failed to see
That there are two sides to this coin.
The chagrin was great because the hope
                        was great.

Why so much hope?
amid the turmoil and confusion - - -
Which did not end - - - - - -
When he was gone.

Was there hope because of the kind of person he was,
Or because a father embodies it?
As a person, my father was an honest man - -
Intelligent - - moral - - basically quite cultured - -
A man who did not fear to look at the world
                                        around him
And to stand up to it
With a courageous intellect.
He fell because he stumbled.
He tripped - - - - - - - - -
On himself.

But many of his positive qualities
I possess myself
Learned from him
With the help of God.

Many of his negative qualities
I do not possess
I could see the error in them
With the help of God.

Surely, God is pleased.
He knows as well as I do - -
That though I'm far from perfect, there is improvement.
My father was the lamb - - the sacrifice
And yet of such heroic stature to match the tragedy
A model to be with,
Even in his distance, compared to fathers nowadays.
I always felt love for him - - - -
Never hate.

THERE WAS A TIME

Thursday, March 9, 1989

There was a time when I was seclusive
Or somehow felt that way
And riding my bike through my neighborhood
Or walking,
I will see a person who is, or seems to be,
Seclusive.
Who gives the impression of having developed
this way,
Throughout life.

There was a time when I was single
And to change that status
To one of being married
Seemed far off indeed.
And, for many years, now,
I have known single people, of all ages,
for whom marriage
seems as remote
As once it was for me.

There was a time
When I was more insecure
Than I am now.
More impatient.
More angry.

There was a time when it would have helped
To take the long view of things
To view life as ongoing,
In various ways.
To see life's trials and upsets and,
Even tragedies
As momentary matters - - - - -
But such an attitude took a while
To sink in.

Aside from the immortality of the soul,
Even death is not the end
In purely human terms.
The deceased, in fact,
Can be seen more clearly,
Understood more easily
Held more closely, more completely
Than before.

Just a few things are important
So few, in fact, that they are difficult
To ferret out.

Such things as being on good terms
With one's self,
In touch with God - - - -
Relating to others - - - - -
Recognizing one's commitments.

So odd to see the eagerness with which
Some people seek to acquire things
Of little importance - - - - - - -
The frenzy with which
Some people seek to acquire things
That are harmful,
Even destructive,
Of spirit and life - -
So little reliance on self exists.

Are we all the same?
Are we similar in the sense that
Once we were each of us lonely - -
Now only some of us are
Once we were all of us blind - -
Now only some of us are
Once we were all of us hyper-dependent - -
Now only some of us are
Once we were all dead in the spirit - -
Now only some of us are.
God's grace unperceived.

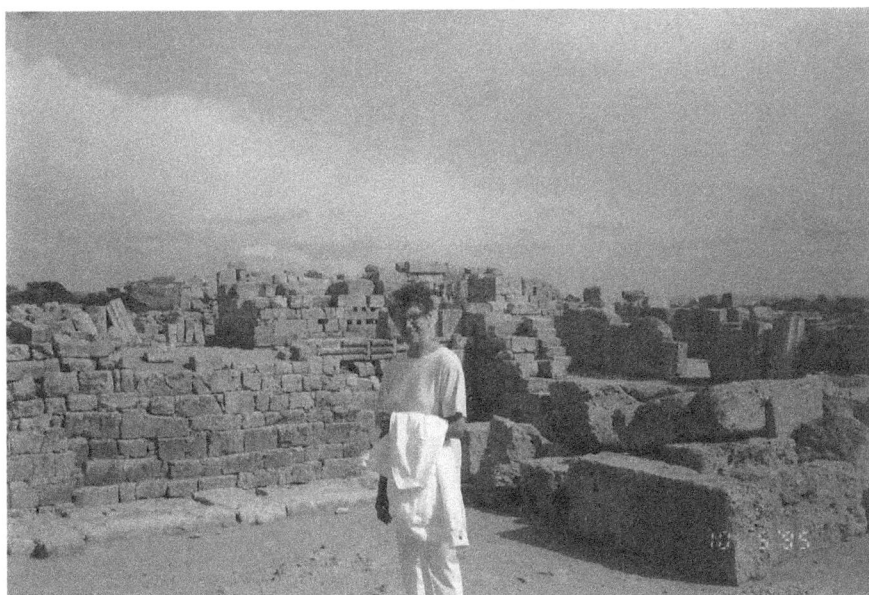

LIFE IS GOOD

Thursday, May 25, 1989

Life is good
And life is its own goodness
And the bloom of life
Is beauty - - - -
And truth.
And love personifies all these things.

And then there is courage
Which ennobles and sustains
And clarifies
And illumines.

AT MY BEST

Tuesday, June 6, 1989

I was perhaps at my best at nine.
That's the time, it seems,
That I go back to, in my mind,
When I want to re-create a time,
When I was simple and straightforward - -
Honest and trusting.

Or was I?
The event that stands out
From that time, occurred,
While, as a family, we were walking home
One night - - - - on Avenue U - - - -
And I noticed a diamond ring
On the sidewalk
And picked it up.

I put it in my pocket
And kept it there until we arrived home,
When I gave it to my mother
Who accepted it, I think,
As a kind of gift of good fortune
With myself as agent.

It was also at nine that Miss Rappaport,
In third grade,
Impressed with my academic ability,
Urged me, in front of the class,
To agree to being advanced a grade - - -
And I expressed a reluctance,
Which was respected.
Nevertheless, this skipping, as it was called,
Was accomplished some years later,
At my mother's fiery and indignant insistence.

Nine is the age I go back to when - - - -
I want to establish a standard for today.
Like how much was a nickel worth to me then - -
And what sum would have equivalence
Today.
Or would fifteen be better - - -
Because at nine, I presume,
I had no money at all.

But when I want to find a time - - -
When there existed a real sense - - - -
Of appreciation,
Of skill - - - - -
Of a fluid alertness - - - - - -
I go back, in my mind's eye,
To the age of twelve - - - - or thirteen
When I played marbles
When hand and eye coordinated to
Shoot an immy out to hit another
And involved immediate feedback
Of success or failure of the enterprise
As well as the ongoingness of the competition.
I try, on occasion, to re-create that feeling
A sense of freedom and accountability intermixed
With skill.

Was it around fourteen
That awkwardness, or out of stepness,
Or something not resembling skill - - - -
And smoothness - - -
Were manifested?
Like that short-lived job as a candy store clerk,
All of two hours long
But, I think the felt experience of awkwardness
Came later,
And stayed - - - - -
And has remained - - - - -
Now a familiar companion.
A precious window, in fact, on life.

But competence came later
At fifteen or sixteen perhaps
In those latter years of high school
When turmoil in the home required
Doing my homework after ten
When everyone else had gone to bed.
There was no time for study as such.
Just the homework assignments.
And a particular mode of attack
On final exams.

Other memories - - - - a sense of things past - - -
Do enter my mind on occasion.
Sometimes I recall that feeling of sanctity
At eleven - - - - -
A time of preparing and receiving
My first holy communion.
And - - - - - I smile
When I see myself as an eight year old,
Having stolen a candy bar - - - - -
And finding myself, soon thereafter,
In the basement
In the most uncomfortable embarrassment
As the storeowner loudly fingered me
To my father upstairs,
My father, in his wisdom,
Never brought it up.

Today is the 45th anniversary of D-Day
The time of the Normandy invasion
I was 24 years old, in London,
Receiving reports of the landing, on radio.
A few weeks later, I would follow - - - - -
And then there would be the St. Lo breakthrough
And the race to Paris
The amazing days with Patton.
The horrors and indignities of war.
The horrors and indignities of concentration camps.
And we struggle to maintain ourselves
We struggle to get a handle on reality,
On truth.

Is that ten or twelve year old important
Because, in his simplicity, there is genuineness?
Because standards are set for the young
To enable them to be the humans
That humans ought to be?
Before the requirements of young adulthood and
The experience of young adulthood
Absorb him and grip him
So that he is no longer free.
Unless, perhaps, somewhere down the road,
He remembers and calls to mind
How once it was.

ARTHUR

Monday, June 19, 1989

Why did my father name me Arthur?
I don't think I ever asked him.
I'm pretty sure of that.
My older brother is named after my father's father.
My middle name is that of my mother's father.
And both my sisters were named
After my father's mother.
Clearly, he had a lot to say about it.

With my naming was begun a new trend.
But, what was its source? - - - - - - - -
Its inspiration.
Was it because it was considered an ancient
                            Roman name?
Or was it because of my date of birth - - - or,
Was I named after the legendary King Arthur,
Of ancient times?
I don't know.

I can see that departures from tradition - - -
Bear explaining.
And with the increasing number of departures - -
From tradition,
A lot more explaining is necessary
If we are to know
What gives - - - -
What's happening.

Even a departure from tradition has a reason.
People look for better-sounding names.
More modern-sounding.
More in tune with present culture.
Salvatore and Domenic are not as common,
Among Italians here,
As they once were.
Nor is Filomena - - - - or Concetta
Even Josephine and Elizabeth.
Aspirations have something to do with it.

Our firstborn received her name from a song
        that was popular at the time.
Jolie Jacqueline.
Her middle name from her maternal grandmother.
Our second had his name discovered - - - -
        after Sunday Mass.
Having asked the priest for a suggestion,
I received a long list at the end of which
Was Stephen.
His middle name derived from mine.
Our third was a compromise,
Gregory having stirred some unpleasant reactions
When I suggested it. So Andrew it was.
The middle name from a boyhood friend who
                had died in the war.
The fourth was Carol - - - steamrollered through
By mother and daughter - - or, I let it happen,
With my mother's Josephine for the middle.

So, that's the record for that generation.
They have their own naming responsibilities
                                        to face - - - -
And to record.
And perhaps to wonder,
With the ensuing years,
Whether the name fits the growing person - - -
Whether the two become simply intertwined,
So that efforts to analyze - - - to discover - - -
Which has the ascendant power
Over the other - - - -
Become moot.

THE MOVING FINGER WRITES

Saturday, June 24, 1989

A thought crossed my mind
As I was shaving this morning.
I had just come off the phone - - - -
With one of my children.

And the usual exchange - - -
There is a usual exchange,
Peculiar to each,
Which lends flavor to life.

In fact, by this time,
I have talked to each of the four
(The two of us have.)
From Alabama to Bakersfield
From Melita to Canoga.

Were circumstances different,
It could be round-the-world
In this mobile age
With families separate
The miracles of communication
Can be utilized
To keep together
That which is stressed apart.

The thought followed upon
An experience of discordance
Or difference of viewpoint
Or philosophy
Or character

Ah yes - - - - - - - - - - - differences.
Yes - - - - - all unique - - - -
Each of us
And God cherishes us - - - -
That's true.

We too can appreciate this uniqueness
This difference
There is strength in us
As we accept each other's differences - - - - -
These peccadillos
These quirks.

And we must accept each other's shortcomings
Despite the toll
We see them take

The thought was in the form
Of a reminder
When in years past - - - - - - -
When I'd hear Bing Crosby sing
Of counting one's blessings
And I, for many years,
Resenting the view
Seeing so little to feel good about.

It took many years - - - - - - - - -
Many, many years
I must have been well into
My forties or fifties - - - -
Maybe even older
Before I began to see
That difficult as it might be,
How necessary it was
To peel back the veneer
Of one's current sorrows
Or anger
Or despair
And see beneath it all
A wealth of blessings.

This morning, though,
I may well be coming full circle
Because I sense an appreciation
For the position I once held
That now I can begin to see
Perhaps in the spirit of the mathematician
That one might count the cost,
(Because there is a cost.)
Sometimes too painful to contemplate,
For all those foibles
These oddities of character and personality.

And, after all,
Is this not in keeping with - - - - -
The tragic view of life - - - - -
That necessary sense of tragedy
Which requires an acceptance
Of tragedy
And as the great tentmaker himself
                    has said
Why presume to undo
What will not be undone
We must
Like God himself
Accept what happens
Even as we sorrow
Over it - - - - - - - - -
But a while.

MICHAEL SMITH

Friday, August 4, 1989

I thought of Michael Smith a few days ago
Father Michael Smith, my friend.
Twelve or thirteen years ago
We'd go to lunch every once in a while.
He was at Our Lady of Grace, Dick's parish,
And I had my office in Encino.
On Ventura.

I thought of him the other day
And yesterday, the Tidings reported his death.
On Monday, July 31st, his 57th birthday.
I have little doubt that my remembering
Was no coincidence.
And if anyone would believe that,
Mike would.
It would be just like him to make the point.

A friend, yes,
He was a friend to me.
I would be pleased to know
That I reciprocated.

He had a keen intelligence.
And self-effacing.
He had two alcoholic fellow priests to deal with.
He would say a lot.
He could be incisive.
And he took on burdens.

A mystery though.
He transferred to the new diocese
In Orange County
And some years ago returned
But I never heard from him.
Strange in that I know we could always pick up
From where we had left off.
And maybe will.
He had it all mapped out.

JACKIE

Sunday, October 1, 1989

You were the first - - - - - -
And the most.

With you, we first became parents - - - - - - - -
And grandparents.

With you we went to church - - - - - -
And choir.

First in school, first in college - - - - - - - -
Happy Birthday, Numero Uno.

love and best wishes,

Mom and Dad

ON THE PLANE TO SPAIN

Saturday, October 7, 1989

Carol was in the hospital
When I saw her last night
But I had to leave.
I had reservations for a trip
To Spain.

She had been somewhat dehydrated
And was still a bit nauseous - - - -
On her second bottle
Of intravenous feeding - - -
But I had to leave
It was nearly ten - - -
And getting up time was three.

I had to see for myself.
This was not the first time.
Real crises.
Close to death a year or so ago
From an unfortunate injection of something - - -
A medical effort that misfired.
Tragedy averted by happenstance - - -
Or God - - -
Or Guardian Angel.

Today's world.
Why so many ills?
Engineered or stumbled into
By the young
And the not so young
And so much medical help to boot.

Stress-filled we are
The gradual increase imperceptible
But its immensity is there
We feel it
Experience it
Talk about it
We cannot escape it.

Even the effort to escape
Is filled with the rigors of stress.
This flight from home
This seeking after relief is,
In this plane,
Thirty-nine thousand feet high,
More stress-filled,
Without let-up
Than anything I know - - - -
And I've known some.

An imbecilic madness.
A mad stupidity.
Inhuman.
De – humanizing.
To be unable to take my human role
My human existence
And see to the important - - - -
The vital
Or, as Don Bosco said,
The necessary.
To do the trivial instead.
The inane.
And, like everyone else,
Or nearly everyone else
To find myself
Admiring the emperor's new clothes.

But, truly,
This is not admiration at all.
I've never felt that way.
El Escorial is only one - - - -
Of many things.
Interesting - - - -
But nothing crucial.

I go along - - - - -
Because I go along
Because to chart my course
Is beyond me
And, to keep to a course
I might chart - - - -
Is beyond me.
The copious input of life today
Crowds out the soul - - - - or - - - -
Pushes it into a corner
The soul oppressed.
Oppressed by input.

The future
The near future just ahead of us
Promises more of the same
The longer range future
May be different.
Who knows.
We may some day,
Somehow,
Solve this problem.

SPAIN

Saturday, October 14, 1989

The rain in Spain flows mainly in the plain.
This time, however, it has been raining,
However uncharacteristically,
On the Costa del Sol - - - -
As we wend our way,
Tour fashion,
Throughout much of Spain.

However much I knew of Spain
Or thought I did,
It was pitifully little.
In fact,
How much can you learn
About anything,
Without experiencing it.

The virgin knows more about virginity
Than the rest of us.
The murderer more about murder
The thief about stealing
A sort of stand-off - - - -
A trade-off.

I had to be in Cordoba
And have a university professor
Be our tour guide,
And for all his faults,
And peccadillos,
In delivery,
To be so vital,
To ask him, privately, why Cordoba was not
More widely known - - - -
For its past greatness - - - -
For its mosques and churches
And synagogues
For its early place in history.
For Seneca
And Maimonides
For its great mosque,
Converted into a cathedral.
I had to be the lone recipient
Of his reply
And see,
And understand
That Spain had some black pages
In its history.

In retrospect,
As you consider the Spaniard - - - -
It seems that Spain
Had to have its particular history.
The turbulence
The suffering
The agony
All of them.
The Christians
The Arabs
The Jews
Intertwined and surging
Back and forth
More interested in building
Than consolidating.
Consolidating only with extremeness
Banishing and obliterating
Pounding and pounding
For centuries.
And the Spaniards won.
They tried it with the Dutch
And failed.
With the English
And crumbled.

And yet they hung in there.
The miracle of Columbus
A vehicle for their greatness,
For their zeal.
They sprang with it
And rushed forth to conquer
Oblivious to his merits - - - -
Envious to the point of treachery.
Little better than the Portuguese.

And here we see laid out before us
Their history
Their traits
Their flamenco
The heel stomping, hand clapping - - -
All to music, guitar and voice
An Arabic moan, or call or yell
Signifying what?
With all its intensity
Its posturing
Orchestrating - - - - improvising
Said to express male virility
Female delicateness.
Really?

The Spaniards have been a great people
They are so appealing - - - -
And so difficult.
Their emphasis on religion is such as
To overwhelm.

They recognize the richness of their endowment.
They developed under the Romans
Acquired a language
And organization.
A tradition of learning
From the Moslems
And wisdom.
And likewise from the Jews
But little of this shows.

Creative and impetuous they have been - - -
And cruel.
Spirited and beautiful - - -
And harsh.
To one another, gentle and friendly,
And murderous.
Filled with religious fervor,
They set out to convert the pagan
Only to end up torturing him in the process
Finding that greed and the search for glory
Had come with them.
Mingling this greed
This need for power
This aesthetic sense
This version of spirituality
To produce enormous monuments
Of silver and gold
And Christ and the Virgin - - - -
God in their own image.

Nations or peoples, like individuals,
Seem to carry traits, like individuals.
Like individuals, perhaps,
But on a larger scale.
The traits are quantitatively larger
And so we have a different meaning - - - -
A different quality.
In fact,
The common trait of individuals in a country
When transformed into a national characteristic
Can become grotesque - - - - -
Once enlisted - - - - -
For the national purpose.

THANK GOD

All Saints Day
Wednesday, November 1, 1989

Thank God for my wife,
Who is my companion.
Who, as companions go,
Is not bad.
Realize, that as companions go,
They, all of them,
Have feet of clay.

One's best friends
For all their friendship - - -
For all their wisdom and strength - - -
For all their constancy and availability
Can be possessed
Of such peccadillos
To make one smile - - - - incredulous.

And friends can be seen,
More or less, at will.
They can be enjoyed
They can be helpful
They can be helped
And when too annoying,
Or, too disappointing
Can give you space
Or you, yourself, take space.

But where spouses are concerned
Though space may be available,
It cannot be of the days kind
Or of weeks, or more.
Rather, life becomes more a crucible
Than a place with gates
For coming and going.

You stay and deal with each other
As best you can - - -
Often poorly.
But marriage is not a passing thing - - -
And you stay.

The years go by
And you stay
And somehow it dawns on you
That you stay,
For a reason - - -
However multifaceted
Or unclear.

The years pass.
The trials continue.
Whether with each other,
Whether over the children,
Or with the outside world
Or whatever - - - -
There is always the necessity,
To deal with each other,
To try to work together,
And failing this,
To continue.

Some people have done it differently.
One friend tells me that
There has never been a disagreement
Or objection.
Or even a harsh word.
I believe it.

In another case
We know people who get along well
And do things together
And yet manage to go, actually,
In separate ways
Quite unconcerned.

And yet another instance
An underlying need
An overt realization or understanding
That disagreement is - - - - - - -
Out of the question.
And something like fear
Holds sway.

There is a certain efficiency in these
That I envy
Also, the decisions.
They seem pretty good - - - - -
And may have caused less pain
Though I'm not sure of this.

Maybe each person lives according to
An internal value system,
At times conscious.
A value system that
Cannot be denied
But is defended.

And so it is with a procedural nod
To the possibility
That here I delude myself
That I express a skepticism
Over the methods mentioned
That look so good
And reasonable.

For freedom and the soul
Are what matter
And freedom is often overlooked
And the soul oppressed.

Neatness of solution,
Success,
Appearance.
These overvalued facets of life
Can rightly be suspect
To the instinct within us.
For instinct senses their cost - - -
If we allow it.

And what now do we have?
Do we have that freedom,
Or some recognition of it?
How bruised,
How beleaguered
The soul?
Has it been valued?
Is there some freedom
And independence?

My life has been littered with a lack of
                    compromise.
Many things endured - - - - -
But little compromise,
In the sense that inner conviction
Has been trampled on.
I have tried to honor conviction
Within myself.

And I have a wife who senses this.
And over the years
We have travailed together,
Rarely sweetly,
But, increasingly, we work
To bring our opinions into some kind
Of harmony
Recognizing more clearly
With the passing years
That our perceptions often coincide
That our goals are essentially the same
That we have so much in common
And that being somewhat in accord
Gives us each the strength
To endure.

For who else on this earthly level
Can know and share the burdens
And the joys,
And all this, in almost constant
Companionship?

WAITING AROUND

Monday, November 13, 1989

I had an idea the other day
For something to write
But it's gone now.

I had quite a few ideas
Piling up
As we came to the end of our trip
In Spain.

And then there was the week in Alabama
And always something would - - - -
Get in the way,
Including indolence
Of one kind or another.

There's nothing like responding to an idea
To inspiration
On the spot.
God is not someone to wait on a person.
He may come back again
But waiting?
No, I don't see him that way.

WALKING

Monday, November 13, 1989

I took a walk this morning
I try to take one every day - - - -
If possible
Usually with my wife
And, usually, we encounter the same scene.
Guard dogs.
Usually Dobermen.

Guard dogs and gated front yards
With locks to prevent entry.

The walk is usually about two miles long
About ten or twelve blocks in all
Only three houses are so guarded.
The first is lived in by a negro fellow
Seems to be a professional
Sometimes a son seems to be there
Once, maybe twice, a woman
Perhaps his wife
Estranged, possibly.

We get along well - - - -
On the few occasions we've seen him.
His guard dogs, he explained,
Are well-trained
They will not bark
They will not attack
Unless someone comes in the gate.
Usually they're out of sight.
I appreciate their quietness.
As well as their out-of-sightedness.

The next example of this fortress mentality
Is just a few houses
Beyond the first.
An immigrant European couple.
Their two Dobermen,
Usually out of sight,
Are not so well-behaved
Their sharp lunges and barking
And snarling
Have forced us to change our path
More than once
In the sight of their owners - - - -
Hopefully, to give them pause - - -
To make them wonder, if perhaps,
Something is not overdone here - - - -
All these protective measures.
They seem like ordinary folk.

The next such instance
About a half block further
Is a place, recently bought,
By some kind of contractor
With large equipment
Behind a newly-constructed high block wall.
It would seem that the enterprise
Is illegal
Being in a residential neighborhood
And the precautions are meant
To conceal.

And so, we take our walks - - - - - -
Some of the few people who do,
And live with a certain amount of unease
But walking harks back to my younger days
Even as a pre-teen
In Brooklyn.
I would not want to do without
The freedom of it
Freedom and peace and spirituality
And getting, also,
A view of the world around us
A feel for the place
The neighborhood
The people
Much appreciated
And much to be appreciated
And loved.

TO BE HUMAN

Saturday, November 18, 1989

Thank God for my father,
Who, in spite of his many faults
And many weaknesses
And sorrows,
Taught me
And all of us
That the committed life
Is the only life
For a human being
That it is the only way
To be human
The only way to live the image
We project on God
The only way to be pleasing to God
So that if God were to ask
What we had done with what
He had given us
We would not have to hang our heads
And admit
That we had sought
Every which way
To run
From our own humanity.

HEALTH CARE

Sunday, November 19, 1989

We belong to the Kaiser Health Plan
The nearest facility of which
Is not far from our home
Less than a couple of miles.

This facility,
Which combines hospital and emergency clinic
Has,
In this day and age
Shared a good bit of our lives.

Whenever something happens,
Like an illness or an accident,
We find ourselves here - - - -
Like this evening,
Mother having severely cut her left middle finger,
Attempting to prepare a lettuce salad.

Carol volunteered to bring her here - - - -
But this being more involved than a cut finger - - - -
I knew
That I would be doing it.

So, we made our way here in the Alfa - - - -
Registration, then waiting room
And soon, the examining room
Which became a surgical room
As the physician-surgeon,
A doctor Mendelson
Administered xylocaine and stitches - - -
Three of them - - -
And it was done.

But, no - - - - - - - - - - - - -
The nurse asked if a tetanus shot
Had been decided upon.
It was.
And now we await its administration.

Eventually,
All the prescribed treatments having been done
The antibiotic salve, for extra security, bought - - -
We made our way home, that night - - - - -
And all this happening against a background,
A very tapestry,
With a multitude of facets,
Or scenes - - - - -
A tapestry of life today
And yesterday.

Aside from the likelihood,
Maybe the fact,
That all this treatment was unnecessary,
We need to acknowledge
That most of the people in this country,
Indeed, the world,
Do not receive this kind of treatment - - - -
Indeed, have no access to it.
They manage without.

(A simple piece of adhesive tape
Would have done the trick
Much as my father did for me,
In three instances that I can remember,
From my childhood.
And never a tetanus shot
Despite the dirt.)

We are less in peril than we think
And those in need often must go it alone
And real need, unheeded, regularly
Brings tragic results.

So, while we view our own needs with
                              special concern
We overlook,
We fail to respond to the needs
              of others.
An ongoing tragedy.

God grant us an awareness of the
                    needs of others,
And a willingness to help
And the means - - - - - -
The modality - - - - -
For helping.

May we have peace
That we may be more likely
To channel our energy
Our intellect
Our compassion - - - -
Toward others, our fellow humans.

Peace first - - - -
Peace without - - - -
Then peace within
So that, thenceforth, our inner peace
            can overflow and flow
                    outward
Into the world.

FAILURE

Tuesday, November 21, 1989

This morning I awoke early
And found myself thinking - - - - -
And this thought crossed my mind:
That I had earlier in this life
Been in situations where I failed to achieve
What I wanted to achieve
At the time.

Disappointed I was
Many times disappointed
Failure has been a good part of my life
Many failures
Some I remember to this day
Even fifty and more years later.

It would be difficult to say
It was all for the better
I've heard that so many times
And, so many times
It seems to have been uttered
More as a platitude
Than anything else.

But I will have to admit - - - - -
I am truly grateful - - - - -
That some of those failures,
The ones I can remember,
The ones I might try to recall,
Perhaps all of them,
For all I know,
Grateful that those failures
Were failures.

This may actually involve
The increasing comfort
The familiarity
The ease
The patience
The acceptance
That one develops within oneself
The improved communing
Perhaps the friendship, too
With oneself
That makes all that has happened
Begin to be more acceptable
Than once it was.
The letting go - - - -
As one grows older.

But not so this morning - - - - -
Not so in specific instances,
When to succeed in a venture
Would seem to have done harm
In some way - - - - -
To myself
And, if others were involved,
To them as well.

How can I begin to list
The many instances of all this
So many they were
They crowd the mind.

For success is a double-edged sword
It comes at a price.

Everything comes at a price
And the greater the success
The greater the price.

Even to become rich
Carries with it the curse,
The misguided view,
Which overvalues riches.

To attain power
To gain renown,
Especially for its own sake,
Is to have participated in a process
Which is falsity personified
And alienates one from others
And from God.

To be alienated from others
And from God
Must involve - - - - - -
An alienation from self
It's all part of the same cloth.

It may be the rare person, if he exists,
Who is totally available
To himself
Some are fortunate
To be moderately present
To themselves
But to be alienated from self
To be unavailable to self
To be not present
Must be to exist
In a graceless prison.

This may all be an exaggeration
But in pursuing this matter in this way
I find myself understanding better
The behavior of people I have known - - - - -
Their behavior over the years.
There have been a number of friendless people
Unable to accept the hand of friendship
Somehow.
Not necessarily bad people
Nor terribly
Or even moderately
Sinful.
But somehow, it seems,
That cringing from failure
Did them in.
And life was bleak - - - -
And death also.

Why do we run from failure - - - - -
Why should it, in our eyes,
Reflect on us
Why need there be so much failure?
Could life not be lived some other way?
Do we instill an orientation towards success
In the young?

Is there some driving force in our civilization,
A need to be an achieving civilization?
A need to justify an existence which,
In God's eyes,
Needs no justification?
Could we do without this?
Could we someday instill into
The fabric of our civilization
The belief - - -
The knowledge - - - -
That failure is every bit as meritorious
　　　　　　　　　　as success,
In most instances,
And even better,
In some?

At this moment,
Communism is crumbling in Europe
A failure.
And some communist chiefs
Are aghast.
And yet this failure is a good thing.
Would that this same view could
　　　　　　　　　　be applied,
In our world,
Across the board.

UNPREDICTABLE

Tuesday, November 21, 1989

In taking my morning walk, this morning,
I came to consider the consolations which,
In walking,
Are available to me.

Initially, there's the freedom in it
First, to be able to make the choice to walk
Also, to have the space to do it in
Like, in this case, the larger neighborhood
And, since one is less protected thereby,
There's the adventure of it
Slight, perhaps, but there nonetheless.

There's the physical freedom, too
The movement through space which,
When confined to a plane, or car,
Or even a home or apartment
Can be more clearly appreciated - - - -
In its absence.

There is a communing with this space
                 around the walker,
Again, not available elsewhere
The nature that surrounds one, on a walk,
Is truly precious
There is nothing like it - - - - - - -
The air, the sometimes freshness of it
The space, and whatever occupies that space
Much of it quite changing and changeable,
Like leaves being moved by the wind - - - - -
Yes, the wind is a factor.

There are apt to others out in that space
That one is walking in
Sometimes no one on a two-mile walk
Or a few walkers themselves
Or maybe dozens, even a hundred, if the
                 neighborhood school - - -
Is having one of its active moments
And some cars too, perhaps a few,
Or even dozens
Each has its driver
A person somehow to consider.

But as I begin to examine
This whole issue of walking
Whose most important
And most cherished aspect has been
The unpredictability of the thoughts
                 that I might have,
Along the way,
I see that this occurs in a setting,
Really,
Of unpredictability
An unpredictability whose influence I had
                 maybe failed to recognize.

In perhaps a vague sort of way
I have had the feeling that walking
And being free in the walking
In the movement of it
And the surprising thoughts in it
The healthiness in it
The capacity in it to resolve thoughts,
And feelings
And directions
Had in it a quality of communing
                with God.

And now I see that God,
With all His structure and structured ways,
Is also the God of the unstructured,
And unpredictable
And that in all this unpredictability
There is something to parallel free will
There is freedom to do,
To change
To develop
And, amazingly,
To find the good, thereby.

In walking,
There is the joy
Of breaking out of the confinement
Of limited physical space
And, sometimes,
The relief of getting away from the
                confining nature of
                    human interaction.

But, increasingly nowadays,
Walking will provide a freedom - - - - - - -
From mankind's machines,
And products,
And games
Which,
Too often,
Serve as a means of vitiating
A person's recognition of the need
For a more realistic contact
With nature,
And with God - - - - -
With other persons, too,
And with his own creativity.

BITTERSWEET

Tuesday, November 21, 1989

There are some things - - - -
That I cannot do anything about

There are limits to the possible - - - -
To the likely

I cannot push myself beyond my limits
Beyond my capacity
Beyond my capability.
And much less can I push someone else.

One of the bittersweet joys of parenthood
Is to come to this conclusion,
Eventually.
To realize that no matter how extensive
            the foolhardiness of one's progeny
No matter the obtuseness,
The sad results - - - - -
However tragic they may be,
That one must come to terms
With the results - - - - -
Sometimes so close to the realm of
                the ridiculous
To make one smile.

They are, after all, in God's hands
And, to quote Msgr. Cosgrove
They become
They are, each one of them
The concern of their guardian angels.

The sweetness lies in the counsel to let go
To surrender the agony
The agonizing
To somehow, some way, give all this to God
Who, we are told,
Despite his infinite burdens,
Will take these on as well.

But on a human level - - - - - - - -
This is difficult to do,
Both because a parent's habit of concern
Is not easily discarded
As well as the need for each of us
To turn to a parent when other resources
            prove to be inadequate
As those of us without living parents
                turn to God
And, on a more immediate and more
                concrete level
To the available priest.

But, as in many or all areas of life
One must seek a balanced view
Seek and maintain, that is.
For bemoaning the sad and negative
Can become a full-time occupation
And can feed on itself.

The joys of parenthood do, in truth, exist,
So easily overlooked though they may be
In the human passion to see the negative
To see it - - - - and not beyond.

For we are creatures of a foolish habit - - - - -
To live in the present
To see the present so greatly magnified
When measured by emotion
That it takes on an importance
Way beyond its merits
Whereas, in fact - - - - - - - - -
We must - - - - - - -
Take the long view.

THE MORNING NEWS

Thursday, December 7, 1989

The TV morning news
It's not on this morning
I didn't turn it on
Preferring for once,
To tune into public radio, KUSC,
Where there is mostly music
And some news
And all so much more pleasant
And human.

No TV news
With its bits and pieces
Meted out.

No TV news
With its desire to be sensational
With a felt need to be sensational
To hold the viewer
Between commercials.

TV news
With its reporters of the news
Not truly reporters in the old sense
But readers of transparent screens
Or windows.

TV news
With its reporters so well paid,
And weather forecasters - - - - -
Would-be meteorologists
Caught, as are the reporters,
Between their astoundingly high pay
The high profile glamour of their roles,
The tenuous nature of their positions
The sometimes seeming importance
Of what they do
The basking in the attention
Of other human beings,
Even, however limited,
A sense of loyalty to the goals,
The aims of journalism
That led them here, some of them,
In the first place
And the corrupting need to lure the viewer,
With inducements
Promises of "more to come"
Insincerity at the service of the advertiser
Insincerity beyond reasonable limits
If insincerity can sometimes qualify
As reasonable.

And does not this insincerity spring from fear
A fear of the loss of all this
Which seems so difficult to foreswear
To relinquish - - - - - - - - - - -
This money
And whatever security money can give
To some
This glory
This being on the main stage
Of the media
This glory, which, however fleeting
Seems momentarily eternal - - - - - - - - -
Such a paradox,
And underlying,
The fear of some abyss, perhaps,
Of loss of all that, somehow,
Has been marketed to them
As important
The opposite end of riches, glory, importance,
A role identity
And instead - - - - - - - -
Poverty, insignificance.

I cannot overlook the fact
That in some way
These are sacrificial lambs - - - - - -
Some deluded
Some not
Who stand by their posts
To reveal the light as best they can
Within the various limits allowed them.

I cannot overlook the fact that - - - - - - -
All of them
Pay a price for all this.
How much they pay
How they pay
Must vary
As each is a variant of sorts
In this regard
As each has his own personality
And perceptions
And each has a different character
A different integrity
A different connection
To the real world around him
To the persons around him.

But almost continually this past year
On those occasions when I've turned
To the morning's TV news
To the three major channels
Switching from one to the other
To avoid the bothersome, ridiculous - - - - - - -
Commercials.
Their noise
Their insult
Their stupid greed
Their disregard for the viewer
And their true responsibility to him
As one must have
Towards any human being
Indeed, any living thing
And, also, the repetitious nature of the news
And the need to estimate if there is truly
This morning
Anything of importance
Of any value
That I might want to see or hear
A judgement I must make
Since the commentators cannot
Or will not do so - - - - - - -
I become irritated, discouraged
Even numb.

Not so this morning
The air seems cleaner
Fresher
My humanity is not trampled upon
By this TV confusion of our times
And its commercials
Its advertisers and hapless presenters.
Not even by the daily newspaper,
Which subscription I let lapse
Three or four years ago,
Nor by commercial radio
With its wild gyrations.
Oh, Lord, how many hapless victims.

No, not this morning
Sitting at my desk I can hear the birds
                              singing
Even in December
My spirit is free
I am in the bosom of God.

AN ARMY ENLISTMENT

Wednesday, December 13, 1989

Fifty years ago, I joined the Army
I enlisted in the "Regular Army"
As they called it
A day or two before my nineteenth birthday.
When I hesitated because of that - - - - -
They signed me up
I took the oath
With the proviso that I receive a 3-day pass
To spend my birthday at home
Which I did.

That was in the latter part of May 1939

My mother had to sign because I was under age

My mother's heart must have been heavy
Yes, there was the possibility of West Point
Which, in fact, came close to happening
And which, surprisingly,
I turned down - - - - - a year later - - - -
Expecting to go home instead
Before the war interfered
But that was an idea - - - - - a thought - - - -
More than anything else.

The motivating factor was the tumult at home
Where there seemed to be no let up
Where a home, leaderless since my father's death
Failed to achieve a balance, a goal
A home wherein my presence seemed increasingly
                    less advisable

And so I left
I simply had to
Or so I thought

Whether it turned out for the better,
                I do not know
There were positives and negatives
Many, I'm sure,
Beyond my ken.

And then again - - - - -
Compared to what?
After all, my remaining at home,
With the tumult reaching ever higher crescendos
Could have been disastrous.

In truth,
We were not a helping society
                    in those days
Or so it seems
There were some systems in place
The Save-a-Life League
Gave some help
An older man — their agent,
A man whose gentle manner
And quiet wisdom
Gave me inspiration
Then and now
But, in spite of our many relatives - - - - -
And friends
There were not the friendship systems
That exist today
The result perhaps of our greater humility
                            today
And quiet wisdom
Beneath the roar of the pace
Of life today.
And the alien materialism
Which propels us all the more
Toward each other.

But I cannot help but grieve over my mother - - - -
The sadness in her life
And the shocks
Especially as I learn better the
           meaning of her admonition to me:
              "Wait until you have children
                 of your own;
                   you'll see."
The awareness of the continuing follies
           of her children
The awareness of tragedy
Tragedy occurring in her adult life
As well as in her childhood
She experienced the eruption of Mt. Vesuvius,
               in Naples
Lava streaming through the streets
And she and her family running before
              the hot stream
The death of her two brothers
And later, the death of her two daughters
Who needed the struggles she had yet to endure?

She had her share of joys, I'm sure
And she could sing
Often of a morning
How many among us, today, have that consolation?
And her children brought her joy
She was so proud of her sons - - - - - - - -
And solicitous.
No one could sing, and cook
    and talk like she did
Who did not have an abundance of life and love
And joy, and courage
The memory of her is a treasured gift.

And for the son in the Army,
And his mother,
There develops an air of poignancy.
The separations
For weeks or months
And more
And distances of hundreds,
And thousands
Of miles
And across the ocean.

A time of maturing for me
The different types of people,
The experiences
The rigors
The training
The actual war - - - - - - - -
Even the concentration camps - - - - - - -
Their living dead
The remnants of the dead
Massive holes for their burial
Stories too unbelievable to tell.

Ships, submarines, planes, trains
London, the channel, Normandy,
Chateaudun, Paris
Belgium, Holland, Germany
Bombs, buzz bombs, shellings,
Strafings, day or night

Captains, majors, colonels, generals,
                    field marshals
The leading actors, their names known
On this most prominent stage - - - - - - -
With the supporting and enabling cast
For this, perhaps the greatest
Event of the century.

A period in my life - - - - - - - - - - - - - -
It started, perhaps, with my enlistment
And ended with my mother's death,
                    January 6, 1946
From nineteen to twenty-five
About six and a half years
Or should I go further back - - - - - - - - -
To my father's death, December 8, 1936
A span of little more than nine years.
A monstrous upheaval
While the whole world shook as well.

And then, again, there are the
                    consolations of faith
                         and perspective.

HEBRON WILSON

Friday, December 22, 1989

I went to confession this evening
Right after a penitential service
I went to Father Hebron Wilson,
A negro priest from Africa.
In these days when black is the term
Advised, required or demanded
While I cling to colored and negro instead
It was so refreshing to hear him say,
From the pulpit,
As he sought to make himself known,
That in his country of Zimbabwe
There were different groups.
One was the coloreds and some others:
"Brown like me"

So Father Wilson is one of the browns.

It seems that from the very beginning
This man was a striking example
Of a man as God would want a man to be
Humble in his strength
Strong in his humility
Quiet, though ready to speak in private
On many issues.

And this readiness to speak applies even to,
Of all places - - - - - - - - -
The confessional.

Father Soto was going through his people - - - - -
Rather rapidly, I thought.
I even grinned inside myself wondering if
Margaret, a truly holy woman,
Had actually gone to confession
It was so fast.

Not so with Father Hebron
And then,
When it came my turn,
I found out why
Although there wasn't much I had to offer
After all, being sixty-nine - - - - - - - -
Was I being quizzical?

He waited - - - - -
He waited me out, perhaps.
He looked at me
(The curtain was drawn back)
He looked at me in his friendly way - - - - - - - -
Silently.

And then he began

The road, he said, is from the Resurrection - - - - -
To Pentecost
And we must travel that road - - - - - - - -
Improving.

No matter the past - - - - - -
Now, in the present - - - - - -
As one improves with age - - - - - -
As one gains in wisdom
One should
Improve further
To the point where
Hurting others - - - even tho done unwittingly - - - -
Will diminish even further.

I thought to say that being that saintly - - - -
As he was,
Would be unattainable.
I'm grateful I said nothing - - - -
Finding myself, instead
Nodding in agreement
As he spoke.

It's a thought.

We'll miss this man.
His bishop, in Africa,
Granted him a six-month extension
To the originally-planned year
And indicated there would be no more.

So be it.
He leaves his mark
In his special way
I hope our paths will cross again.

PREVIOUS BOOKS BY THE AUTHOR

Unlike the Vikings

Casta Diva

GrandMa and the Miracles

The Bird and the Squirrel

Rosalie Was All Night Without the Light

Chocolate and Cigarettes

The Snow Was Falling

The Issue

RIVERSHORE BOOKS

Website:
www.rivershorebooks.com

Blog:
blog.rivershorebooks.com

Facebook:
www.facebook.com/rivershore.books

Twitter:
www.twitter.com/rivershorebooks

Email:
Info@rivershorebooks.com

www.ingramcontent.com/pod-product-compliance
Lightning Source LLC
Chambersburg PA
CBHW031628040426
42452CB00007B/722